Prudence Marshall
'Trees',
Wombourne Road,
Trysull.
WV5 7JB

G.L.A.D.

A

Pony Rider's

D   I   A   R   Y

This Diary Belongs To:

Prudence Marshall.

19___

A

Pony Rider's

D I A R Y

Nina Duran

Robert Hale □ *London*

To Nona Garson,

my friend and trainer

who understands ponies

better than anyone I know

and to Popcorn . . .

ISBN   0–7090–3581–0

Robert Hale Limited
Clerkenwell House
Clerkenwell Green
London EC1R OHT

Printed in Japan

Contents

Introduction

*W**ithout fail, that first mo-*
ment—when I'm going to visit my hunter at the farm or
I pass a carriage horse in the park and just catch that
horsey scent in the air—I'm always brought back to my
Popcorn days. Popcorn permitted my first ride on a
Saturday morning, with my brother and father watch-
ing. He was ancient and, looking back, unbelievably
tolerant. Hanging onto his very full mane, I was
bounced around the ring a few times, giggling with
delight. He very kindly stopped at the gate, waited
quietly while I was lifted off by my father, and proceeded
to pin his ears flat on his head. He looked fierce, but I
understood him perfectly. Out came a piece of sugar from
my pocket, and his ears perked up. He got his thank you.
From then on I was hooked.

Many of the world's outstanding riders got their start
on a pony, taking endless turns around the ring trying to
keep the pony from drifting toward the centre (an

invaluable, early lesson in leg aids), learning the art of perseverance on an animal that offers no shortcuts. Watching a seasoned pony carry its young rider, one senses that the pony is doing the teaching. With an uncanny sense of a rider's limitations and often genuine kindness, ponies seem to possess an intelligence you don't always see in horses.

Ponies also have a superior sense of balance, owing to their lower centre of gravity, and pound for pound seem to be better athletes than horses. It is amazing to see a pony accomplish horse-size feats, and after riding horses for years now, I'm still amazed by how good ponies are.

They seem to come in two varieties. There are the wise, ancient ponies like Popcorn—the sage "belly splinter" ponies that tuck their legs up to their chin when they jump, ears pricked, taking care. They are the ponies that have taught the mothers and now carry the daughters, that keep moving often into their thirties, the only difference being that they are perhaps a bit more set in their ways. But, however stubborn, they remain unflappable, like Lancer, the flea-bitten grey who's taught nearly every-

body at my yard. He's impossible to flex or bend, but he knows the instructor's words by heart and canters on command, giving the rider a thrilling sense of accomplishment that may be false but still builds confidence.

Then there are the imps, the ponies who teach you the art of falling off ("That's yours now," the instructor would say, pointing to the patch of ground I'd landed on.) Pretty Boy was my first fall. And sweet Timmy, a tiny dappled grey, perks up whenever he sees a jump in front of him. He loves to go fast, and the rider who doesn't see his eyes suddenly go bright with anticipation will have a handful in a moment.

But there is a lovely little mare named Rosie at the barn who's the ideal. Neither an ancient nor an imp but a little bit of both, she's a quality pony who's taught her young owner kindness, courage, and a deep sense of responsibility. They adore each other. Rosie always gives her all and never misses in the ring, and her rider concentrates with a child's intensity. It's no wonder they've won so many ribbons. They're a beautiful picture.

— N.D.

My Pony's Vital Statistics

Registered show name _MAY DAY BOY._

Stable _'TREES' TRYSULL EBBTREES._

Breed _COB WELSH (NOT QUITE SURE)_

Colour/Markings _4 WHITE CORONETS + BLAZE._

Height _14·2_

Year of birth 19 _84_

Date of purchase _1 · 9 · 90 ._

Sire _____

Dam _____

Insurance company/Broker _Duvaxyn/HORSESENSE_

Policy number _HP17866 ._

Type of cover _SECTIONS 1 – 10 ._

Insured value:

   Pony _£1000 ._

   Tack _£750_

Renewal dates _07/10/1991 ._

Freeze mark number _____

My Pony's Stable

Name Marshall.

Address of stable 'Trees', Woumbourne Road.

Telephone number 0902 896759.

Stable or yard owner Sarah and Prudence.

Yard manager " " " "

Instructors Louise

Grooms ME!

The People Who Look
After My Pony

Groom(s)

   Telephone number(s)

Veterinarian DAVID FRANKLIN

   Telephone number 25 26234 | CAR PHONE 0860 -527342.

Farrier Tim Budd.

   Telephone number 700 969.

My Pony's Feeding Schedule

Morning: nuts spillers or/CHAFF & MIX & SUGA

Type and quantity of feed ~~sometimes change feed routines.~~

Hay (quantity) 1 section (soaked if he gets a cough).

Afternoon:

Type and quantity of feed 1 scoop mixed nuts/ (in winter add chaff etc)

Hay (quantity) 1 section.

Special instructions ALWAYS ADD WATER TO HIS FOOD OTHERWISE HE WILL GET A COUGH.

Farrier and Veterinary Care

Farrier _Tim Budd._

Shoeing (Note dates pony is due to be shod):

January _Shoed._   July _Shoed_

February _____   August _____

March _Shoed._   September _Shoed_

April _____   October _____

May _Shoed_   November _Shoed_

June _____   December _____

Special care _____

Veterinary check/Treatment _____

Grooming and Stable Supplies

- ☑ *Dandy brush*
- ☑ *Body brush*
- ☑ *Water brush*

metal ☑ *Curry combs*
- ☑ *Mane / Tail combs*
- ☑ *Hoofpick*

- ☑ *Sweat scraper*
- ☑ *Sponges*
- ☑ *Towels*
- ☑ *Fly spray*
- ☑ *Hoof oil*

Other items:
- ☐ *Liniment*
- ☑ *Wound powder*
- ☑ *Poultice*
- ☑ *Water buckets*
- ☑ *Shampoo*
- ☑ *Hay net*

elastic bands (brown)

Saddle _Pennwood Elite General Purp ._

Size _____

Girth size _Cob_____

Bit (s) _Kimblewick & Snaffle ._

Bridle/Martingale _Pennwood Forge ._

Halter:

Size _____

Colour _____

Stable rug:

Size _MEDIUM_

Colour _BLUE_

Turnout rug:

Size _____

Colour _____

Sweat rug:

Size _BLUE WITH RED_

Colour _____

My Riding Clothes

Helmet or hat size **6 ⅜**

Shirt:

    Size _____

    Colours _____

Jacket:

    Size _____

    Colours _____

Jodhpurs:

    Size **Black** _____

    Colour _____

    Boot size _____

Gloves:

    Size _____

    Colour _____

My Riding Friends

Owner/Rider _Jenny Shanks._

Telephone number _____

Pony's name _Sovereign / Flash._

Owner/Rider _Victoria Young_

Telephone number _743347 ._

Pony's name _Sorrell + Dora_

Owner/Rider _Julia Corns._

Telephone number _____

Pony's name _____

My Favourite Riders
(and why I admire them)

Name ~~Micheal~~ Whitakker on
Henderson Milton because he is great.

Name

Name

My Favourite Ponies
(and why I like them)

Pony's name Fizz - because he knows that I'm his mom and I ♡ him.

Pony's name Maxwell - because he reminds me of Candy.

Pony's name Sweet Jamie - because he's got a real character.

Harry because he's mine
Same as Fizz (but Harry's better).

My Favourite Horse Stories, Books, and Films

Title Blackbeauty, Fly by Night
Flying Changes, Year of the Black-
Title Pony. Darkling

Title _____

My Local Pony Club

Name *Albrighton Hunt.*

District

Location

Secretary's name

Secretary's telephone number

Instructor's name

Instructor's telephone number

My membership number

Membership renewal date

Annual events

My Training Schedule

Instructor <u>Sarah -Jayne</u>

Things we worked on <u>Jumping,</u>

<u>Flying Changes, 3 Flying</u>

<u>Changes.</u>

Things to practise on my own (and to remember)

My Training Schedule

Instructor _Louise_

Things we worked on Flying Changes, turn on the quart hindes, Rein back.

Things to practise on my own (and to remember)

My Training Schedule

*Instructor*_____

*Things we worked on*_____

_____

_____

_____

_____

_____

*Things to practise on my own (and to remember)*_____

_____

_____

_____

_____

_____

My Training Schedule

*Instructor*_____ _____

*Things we worked on*_____

_____

_____

_____

_____

_____

*Things to practise on my own (and to remember)*_____

_____

_____

_____

_____

_____

☐ My Training Schedule ☐

*Instructor*_____

*Things we worked on*_____

_____

_____

_____

_____

_____

*Things to practise on my own (and to remember)*_____

_____

_____

_____

_____

_____

My Training Schedule

*Instructor*_____

*Things we worked on*_____

_____

_____

_____

_____

_____

*Things to practise on my own (and to remember)*_____

_____

_____

_____

_____

_____

My Training Schedule

*Instructor*_____

*Things we worked on*_____

_____

_____

_____

_____

_____

*Things to practise on my own (and to remember)*_____

_____

_____

_____

_____

_____

My Training Schedule

*Instructor*_____ _____ _____

*Things we worked on*_____ _____

_____ _____ _____ _____

_____ ____ _____ ____ ___

_____ _____ _____ ____ __

_____ ____ _____·_____

_____ _____

*Things to practise on my own (and to remember)*_____

___ _____ _____

_____ _____

_____ _____ ___

_____ __ _____

_____ _____

My Training Schedule

*Instructor*_____

*Things we worked on*_____

_____

_____

_____

_____

_____

*Things to practise on my own (and to remember)*_____

_____

_____

_____

_____

_____

My Training Schedule

*Instructor*_____ _____

*Things we worked on*_____ _____

_____

_____

_____

_____

_____

*Things to practise on my own (and to remember)*_____

_____

_____

_____

_____

_____

Horse Show Checklist

Grooming equipment:
- ✓ Dandy brush
- ✓ Body brush
- ✓ Water brush
- ✓ Curry combs
- ✓ Hoofpick
- ✓ Sweat scraper

- ✓ Sponges
- ✗ Towels
- ✗ Quarter markers
- ✗ Fly spray
- ✓ Hoof oil

Plaiting equipment:
- ✗ Combs
- ✗ Scissors
- ✗ Rubber bands/Needles and thread/Yarn
- ✗ Step ladder/Stool

Sundry items:
- ✓ Water bucket
- ✓ Hay net
- ✗ Feed

Horse Show Checklist

My pony's tack and clothing:

☑ Saddle   ☑ Bridle

☑ Numnah   ☒ Breastplate

☑ Martingale   ☑ Tail bandage

☑ Girth   ☒ Crupper

☑ Travel bandages   ☑ Brush boots

☑ Leg bandages   ☑ Sweat rug

☒ Halter   ☒ Exercise blanket

☑ Lead rope   ☒ Roller

☒ Lunge line   Summer sheet.

My riding clothes:

☑ Hat/Helmet   ☑ Gloves

☑ Shirt (and stock or tie)   ☑ Crop

☑ Jacket   ☑ Spurs

☑ Jodphurs   ☑ Hairnet

☑ Boots   ☑ Waterproofs

The Gymkhana □

The Gymkhana

Name of show _____

Date _____

Event name _____

Pony's name _____

Entry number _____

Entry fee _____

Result _____

Prize money _____

The Gymkhana

Name of show _____

Date _____

Event name _____

Pony's name _____

Entry number _____

Entry fee _____

Result _____

Prize money _____

The Gymkhana

Name of show _____

Date _____

Event name _____

Pony's name _____

Entry number _____

Entry fee _____

Result _____

Prize money _____

The Gymkhana

Name of show _____

Date _____

Event name _____

Pony's name _____

Entry number _____

Entry fee _____

Result _____

Prize money _____

The Gymkhana

Name of show _____

Date _____

Event name _____

Pony's name _____

Entry number _____

Entry fee _____

Result _____

Prize money _____

The Gymkhana

Name of show _____

Date _____

Event name _____

Pony's name _____

Entry number _____

Entry fee _____

Result _____

Prize money _____

The Gymkhana

Name of show _____

Date _____

Event name _____

Pony's name _____

Entry number _____

Entry fee _____

Result _____

Prize money _____

The Gymkhana

Name of show _____

Date _____

Event name _____

Pony's name _____

Entry number _____

Entry fee _____

Result _____

Prize money _____

The Gymkhana

Name of show _____

Date _____

Event name _____

Pony's name _____

Entry number _____

Entry fee _____

Result _____

Prize money _____

The Gymkhana

Name of show _____

Date _____

Event name _____

Pony's name _____

Entry number _____

Entry fee _____

Result _____

Prize money _____

The Gymkhana

Name of show _____

Date _____

Event name _____

Pony's name _____

Entry number _____

Entry fee _____

Result _____

Prize money _____

The Gymkhana

Name of show _____ ___ _____

Date _____ _____ ___

Event name _____ ___ ___ _____

Pony's name _____ _____ __

Entry number _____ _____

Entry fee _____ __

Result _____ _

Prize money _____ _____ __

The Gymkhana

Name of show _____

Date _____

Event name _____

Pony's name _____

Entry number _____

Entry fee _____

Result _____

Prize money _____

The Gymkhana

Name of show _____

Date _____ _____ ___

Event name _____ _____ ___

Pony's name _____ _____ ___

Entry number _____

Entry fee _____

Result __ _____

Prize money __ _____ _____

The Gymkhana

Name of show _____

Date _____

Event name _____

Pony's name _____

Entry number _____

Entry fee _____

Result _____

Prize money _____

The Gymkhana □

Name of show _____

Date _____

Event name _____

Pony's name _ _____

Entry number _____

Entry fee _____

Result _____

Prize money _____

The Gymkhana

Name of show _____

Date _____

Event name _____

Pony's name _____

Entry number _____

Entry fee _____

Result _____

Prize money _____

The Gymkhana

Name of show _____

Date _____

Event name _____

Pony's name _____

Entry number _____

Entry fee _____

Result _____

Prize money _____

The Gymkhana

Name of show _____

Date _____

Event name _____

Pony's name _____

Entry number _____

Entry fee _____

Result _____

Prize money _____

The Gymkhana

Name of show _____

Date _____

Event name _____

Pony's name _____

Entry number _____

Entry fee _____

Result _____

Prize money _____

The Gymkhana

Name of show _____

Date _____

Event name _____

Pony's name _____

Entry number _____

Entry fee _____

Result _____

Prize money _____

The Gymkhana

Name of show _____

Date _____

Event name _____

Pony's name _____

Entry number _____

Entry fee _____

Result _____

Prize money _____

The Gymkhana ❑

Name of show _____

Date _____

Event name _____

Pony's name _____

Entry number _____

Entry fee _____

Result _____

Prize money _____

□ The Horse Show □

The Horse Show

Name of show _COSFORD RMAS SHOW._

Date _15/12/90._

Location _COSFORD_

Indoor/Outdoor _INDOOR._

Show rating _____

Travelling cost _:_____

Show requirement _____

Registration number _____.____

Height measurement number _MIXED_

Section _____

Class entered _TOP SCORE   Jump off._

Entry fee _free_

Rider's fee _free._

Judge _Don't know._

Results/Placing _Terrible_

Trophy _none_

Prize money _none_

Comments _he just would not jump._

The Horse Show

Name of show _WOLVERLY AND DISTRICT._

Date _24·3·91_

Location _WOLVERLY._

Indoor/Outdoor _Outdoor._

Show rating _Grade C._

Travelling cost _?_

Show requirement _Dressage/Jumping 1._

Registration number _?_

Height measurement number _14·2½._

Section _?_

Class entered _O·D·E._

Entry fee _£5   (member fee)._

Rider's fee _?_

Judge _R·J·Seymore._

Results/Placing _3rd Dressage / 2nd O·D·E._

Trophy _2nd._

Prize money _£10_

Comments _Good for first O·D·E on Harry since xmas._

The Horse Show

*Name of show*_____

*Date*_____

*Location*_____

*Indoor/Outdoor*_____

*Show rating*_____

*Travelling cost*_____

*Show requirement*_____

*Registration number*_____

*Height measurement number*_____

*Section*_____

*Class entered*_____

*Entry fee*_____

*Rider's fee*_____

*Judge*_____

*Results/Placing*_____

*Trophy*_____

*Prize money*_____

*Comments*_____

_____

The Horse Show

Name of show _____

Date _____

Location _____

Indoor/Outdoor _____

Show rating _____

Travelling cost _____

Show requirement _____

Registration number _____

Height measurement number _____

Section _____

Class entered _____

Entry fee _____

Rider's fee _____

Judge _____

Results/Placing _____

Trophy _____

Prize money _____

Comments _____

The Horse Show

*Name of show*_____ _____

*Date*_____

*Location*_____

*Indoor/Outdoor*_____

*Show rating*_____

*Travelling cost*_____

*Show requirement*_____

*Registration number*_____

*Height measurement number*_____ _____

*Section*_____

*Class entered*_____ _____

*Entry fee*_____

*Rider's fee*_____

*Judge*_____

*Results/Placing*_____

*Trophy*_____

*Prize money*_____

*Comments*_____

_____

The Horse Show

*Name of show*_____

*Date*_____

*Location*_____

*Indoor/Outdoor*_____

*Show rating*_____

*Travelling cost*_____

*Show requirement*_____

*Registration number*_____

*Height measurement number*_____

*Section*_____

*Class entered*_____

*Entry fee*_____

*Rider's fee*_____

*Judge*_____

*Results/Placing*_____

*Trophy*_____

*Prize money*_____

*Comments*_____

The Horse Show

*Name of show*_____

*Date*_____

*Location*_____

*Indoor/Outdoor*_____

*Show rating*_____

*Travelling cost*_____

*Show requirement*_____

*Registration number*_____

*Height measurement number*_____

*Section*_____

*Class entered*_____

*Entry fee*_____

*Rider's fee*_____

*Judge*_____

*Results/Placing*_____

*Trophy*_____

*Prize money*_____

*Comments*_____

_____

The Horse Show

Name of show _____

Date _____

Location _____

Indoor/Outdoor _____

Show rating _____

Travelling cost _____

Show requirement _____

Registration number _____

Height measurement number _____

Section _____

Class entered _____

Entry fee _____

Rider's fee _____

Judge _____

Results/Placing _____

Trophy _____

Prize money _____

Comments _____

The Horse Show

Name of show _____

Date _____

Location _____

Indoor/Outdoor _____

Show rating _____

Travelling cost _____

Show requirement _____

Registration number _____

Height measurement number _____

Section _____

Class entered _____

Entry fee _____

Rider's fee _____

Judge _____

Results/Placing _____

Trophy _____

Prize money _____

Comments _____

The Horse Show

Name of show _____

Date _____

Location _____

Indoor/Outdoor _____

Show rating _____

Travelling cost _____

Show requirement _____

Registration number _____

Height measurement number _____

Section _____

Class entered _____

Entry fee _____

Rider's fee _____

Judge _____

Results/Placing _____

Trophy _____

Prize money _____

Comments _____

_____

The Horse Show □

Name of show _____

Date _____

Location _____

Indoor/Outdoor _____

Show rating _____

Travelling cost _____

Show requirement _____

Registration number _____

Height measurement number _____

Section _____

Class entered _____

Entry fee _____

Rider's fee _____

Judge _____

Results/Placing _____

Trophy _____

Prize money _____

Comments _____

The Horse Show

Name of show _____

Date _____

Location _____

Indoor/Outdoor _____

Show rating _____

Travelling cost _____

Show requirement _____

Registration number _____

Height measurement number _____

Section _____

Class entered _____

Entry fee _____

Rider's fee _____

Judge _____

Results/Placing _____

Trophy _____

Prize money _____

Comments _____

The Horse Show

Name of show _____

Date _____

Location _____

Indoor/Outdoor _____

Show rating _____

Travelling cost _____

Show requirement _____

Registration number _____

Height measurement number _____

Section _____

Class entered _____

Entry fee _____

Rider's fee _____

Judge _____

Results/Placing _____

Trophy _____

Prize money _____

Comments _____

_____

The Horse Show

Name of show _____

Date _____

Location _____

Indoor/Outdoor _____

Show rating _____

Travelling cost _____

Show requirement _____

Registration number _____

Height measurement number _____

Section _____

Class entered _____

Entry fee _____

Rider's fee _____

Judge _____

Results/Placing _____

Trophy _____

Prize money _____

Comments _____

_____

The Horse Show

Name of show _____

Date _____

Location _____

Indoor/Outdoor _____

Show rating _____

Travelling cost _____

Show requirement _____

Registration number _____

Height measurement number _____

Section _____

Class entered _____

Entry fee _____

Rider's fee _____

Judge _____

Results/Placing _____

Trophy _____

Prize money _____

Comments _____

_____

The Horse Show

Name of show _____

Date _____

Location _____

Indoor/Outdoor _____

Show rating _____

Travelling cost _____

Show requirement _____

Registration number _____

Height measurement number _____

Section _____

Class entered _____

Entry fee _____

Rider's fee _____

Judge _____

Results/Placing _____

Trophy _____

Prize money _____

Comments _____

▫ The Horse Show ▫

Name of show _____

Date _____

Location _____

Indoor/Outdoor _____

Show rating _____

Travelling cost _____

Show requirement _____

Registration number _____

Height measurement number _____

Section _____

Class entered _____

Entry fee _____

Rider's fee _____

Judge _____

Results/Placing _____

Trophy _____

Prize money _____

Comments _____

_____

The Horse Show

Name of show _____

Date _____

Location _____

Indoor/Outdoor _____

Show rating _____

Travelling cost _____

Show requirement _____

Registration number _____

Height measurement number _____

Section _____

Class entered _____

Entry fee _____

Rider's fee _____

Judge _____

Results/Placing _____

Trophy _____

Prize money _____

Comments _____

_____

My Ambitions with
Ponies and Horses

My Ambitions with Ponies and Horses

My ambitions are to win an Olympic driving class.
And breeds arabs and Caspians.

This Is a Picture of My Favourite Pony

A Pony Rider's Diary

Composed in Caslon 540 Roman and Italic

Designed by Danielle Sacripante

Prudence
Marshall!